THE COMPLETE KWANZAA CELEBRATION BOOK

1

Published by:
Creative Acrylic Concepts
5792 Kensington Road
Detroit, Michigan 48224

First edition, 1993.
Revised edition, 1994

Designs & Illustrations by:
Ronald Rutherford.

Manufactured in the United States of America

Library of Congress Catalog Card Number: 94-92261

ISBN: 0-9639026-8-7

Song: WE SHALL OVERÇOME
Musical and Lyrical adaptation by Zilphia Horton, Frank Hamilton, Guy Carawan and Pete Seeger. Inspired by African American Gospel Singing, members of the Food & Tobacco Workers Union, Charleston, SC, and the southern Civil Rights Movement.
TRO (c) Copyright 1960 (Renewed) and 1963 (Renewed) Ludlow Music, Inc., New York, NY.
Royalities derived from this composition are being contributed to the We Sall Overcome Fund and The Freedom Movement under the Trusteeship of the writers.
Used by Permission.

Song: Keep Your Eyes On The Prize
A freedom song version of the old spiritual "Mary Had A Golden Chain". From: Songs of Peace, Freedom and Protest: collected and edited with notes by Tom Glazer, Fawcett Publication, 1972.

THE COMPLETE KWANZAA CELEBRATION BOOK

by
Linda Robertson

Publishers
Creative Acrylic Concepts
Detroit, Michigan 48224

RAP

"A PEOPLE WITHOUT THE KNOWLEDGE OF THEIR PAST HISTORY, ORIGIN AND CULTURE IS LIKE A TREE WITHOUT ROOTS".

MARCUS GARVEY

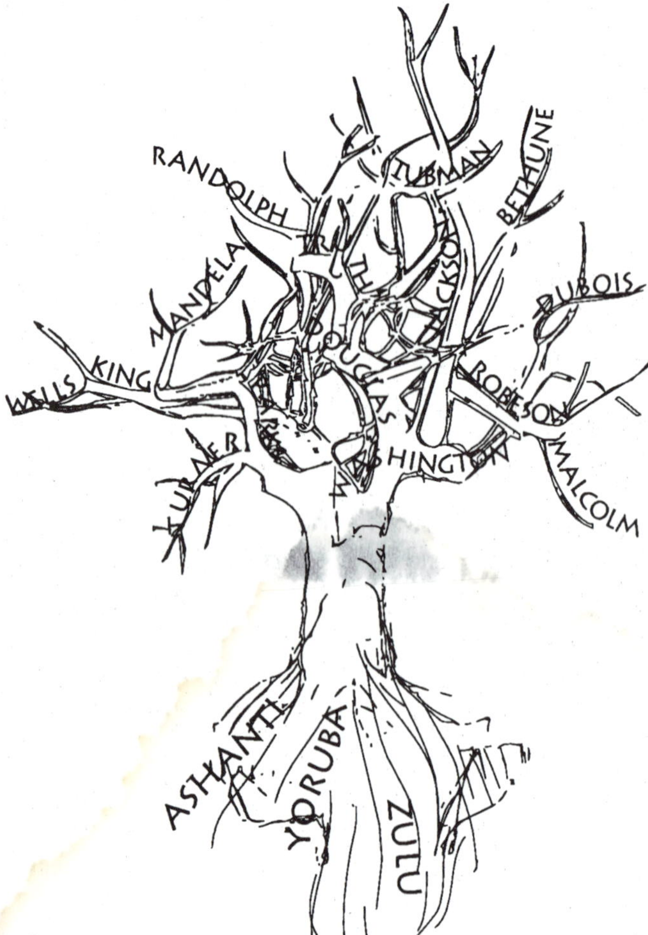

ACKNOWLEDGMENTS

The development and production of this book started with an idea to create a gift basket commemorating KWANZAA. As the gift basket evolved it became clear that most African Americans supported the concept of KWANZAA, but many were not sure how to plan or carry out a KWANZAA celebration.

Our work then shifted from what was originally a two–page brochure describing the seven principles of KWANZAA to a 80–page instructional, how to have a KWANZAA celebration book. The result, we feel, is a perfect synergy of the philosophy of KWANZAA with the functional items needed to perform the ceremonies.

To everyone involved–Thank you, but most especially to:
Norma Davis, editor extraordinaire, who at a moment's notice took on the task of turning my scribbles into readable and grammatically correct sentences.
Ron Rutherford, "Young man on the way up," for all of the marvelous illustrations and designs.
Shirley Jackson, for the feedback and encouragement on the book, the basket and everything in between.
El-Ra, for sharing the African designs that border the front cover. The staff at Kinko's printing in Detroit and in Grosse Pointe and the men and women at the College of Lifelong Learning at Wayne State University.

Years ago, I received a plaque that said, "Life's greatest treasures are found in the friendship we make along the way." I know of nothing truer. Thank you, Barbara Miller and Joseph Miller, for being two of my great treasures. Thanks also to Deborah Payne for her enormous source of strength and vision; to my prayer partner, Jerry Barker, who consistently adds to the quality of my life; and to my mother, Ella Robertson and my brother Reginald.

And to my Life Supports–Omar Car, Vina Price, Booker Fullilove, Carol Crawford, Alex Bailey, Mozella Garrett and family, and Mrs. Lee Mason.

There is a movement being rekindled among African Americans–a movement to reclaim, restore and revive our cultural heritage and to reject the false idols of materialism and moral decay.

The celebration of KWANZAA, a cultural holiday created by an African American and sanctioned by the African American community is an important link to this movement.

Kwanzaa, the only nationally celebrated indigenous, non-heroic African American holiday, offers our children a rich and noble legacy

to learn from

to add to and strengthen

and

to pass on to the next

generations.

Thank you, Maulana Ron Karenga, for your insight, wisdom, courage and love of self and love of your people.

DEDICATION

To all my ancestral spirits that have gone before me, but especially to: My father, Robert Robertson, and my grandmother, Florine Chisholm, who gave me generous portions of unconditional love and support.

My grandmother's sister, my Aunt Eliza, who offered to all who knew her the lessons of courage and boldness.

My Aunt Frances, who was not my aunt through kinship, but surely through love, who never forgot any of my birthdays or any other occasion to celebrate me.

I lift up the libation cup to you all in grace and in gratitude.

TABLE OF CONTENTS

THE BASICS
History.......11
The Seven Principles.......13
KWANZAA Symbols.......15
KWANZAA Ceremonies.......17
Gifts.......20

THE SCENE
Ambience.......23
Protocol.......24

PREPARATION
CheckList.......31
Program Booklet.......34
Do's and Don'ts.......35

KWANZAA & CHILDREN
Things Children Can Do.......39
Things Children Can Make.......44

KWANZAA YEAR-ROUND
Unity.......48
Self Determination.......51
Collective Work And Responsibility.......53
Cooperative Economics.......55
Purpose.......57
Creativity.......59
Faith.......61

APPENDIX
Sample Karamu Program.......65
Sample Program Booklet.......66
Songs
  We Shall Overcome.......68
  Keep Your Eyes On The Prize.......70
Sample Libation Statement.......72
Sample Farewell Statment.......72

BIBLIOGRAPHY.......73
INDEX.......74

THE BASICS

"KNOWLEDGE IS THE PRIME NEED OF THE HOUR."

MARY MCLEOD BETHUNE

THE COMPLETE KWANZAA CELEBRATION BOOK

HISTORY

KWANZAA was created in 1966 by Dr. Maulana Karenga, founder and chairman of the Black Nationalist Organization, "US". KWANZAA is a cultural holiday that introduces and establishes principles and practices designed to recapture the essence of our African American selves and to give our children a positive Afrocentric value system for the future. KWANZAA is observed from December 26 through January 1st.

The word KWANZAA comes from the Swahili word, Kwanza, which means first and is part of the phrase Matunda Ya Kwanza (which means first fruits). The traditional African practice of gathering together to celebrate the harvest of the first crops/fruits served as the inspiration for the African American holiday. Dr. Karenga added the extra "a" to KWANZA to distinguish the African American holiday from the African word, but the same concept of gathering and celebration forms the basis for the KWANZAA celebration.

THUS, KWANZAA IS A TIME FOR:

- the gathering in of our people,
- the celebration of ourselves and our achieve ments, and
- the renewal and reaffirmation of our commitment to positive values (The Seven Principles).

THE NGUZO SABA

(En-GOO-Zoh-Sah-BAH)

THE SEVEN PRINCIPLES

The NGUZO SABA represents the minimum set of principles by which African Americans should live. They are social principles (values) and deal with how we should relate to one another and how we should build our lives and our future. The Nguzo Saba requires us to act in accordance with our highest good and the highest good of our people.

The Seven Principles Are:

UMOJA (oo-MOE-jah) UNITY
To strive for and maintain unity in the family, community, nation and race.

KUJICHAGULIA (koo-jee-cha-goo-LEE-ah) SELF DETERMINATION
To define ourselves, name ourselves, create for ourselves and speak for ourselves, instead of being defined, named, created for, and spoken for by others.

UJIMA (oo-JEE-mah) COLLECTIVE WORK & RESPONSIBILITY
To build and maintain our community together and to make our sisters' and brothers' problems our problems and to solve them together.

UJAMAA (oo-JAH-mah) CO-OPERATIVE ECONOMICS

To build and maintain our own stores, shops and other businesses and to profit from them together.

NIA (nee-AH) PURPOSE

To make as our collective vocation the building and developing of our community in order to restore our people to their traditional greatness.

KUUMBA- (koo-OOM-bah) CREATIVITY

To always do as much as we can, in the way we can, in order to leave our community more beautiful and beneficial than when we inherited it.

IMANI (ee-MAH-nee) FAITH

To believe with all our hearts in our people, our parents, our teachers, our leaders and the righteousness and victory of our struggle.

KWANZAA SYMBOLS

Like other important holidays, KWANZAA has its special symbols. The symbols are instructional in that they represent and reinforce the basic principles and concepts of KWANZAA.

1. Mkeka - (M-kay-cah) A straw or African textile mat that represents our African traditions. The Mkeka symbolizes the foundation on which all else rests and the foundation upon which we build.

2. Kinara - (Kee-nah-rah) A seven-place candle-holder that represents the original stalk from which we all sprang. It also represents reason and social structure.

3. Mishumaa Saba - (Mee-shoo-maah sah-bah) The seven candles;–one black, three red, and three green, which represent the Seven Principles (Nguzo Saba), the heart of the KWANZAA value system.

4.Mazao - (Mah-zah-oh) The fruits and vegetables that symbolize the rewards of collective labor and also symbolize the historical roots of the holiday as a time of joy and togetherness.

5. *Vibunzi (Vi-bun-zi) Ears of corn, the Vibunzi symbolize children; thus, each family displays as many ears of corn as it has children. Note, even households with no children should place an ear of corn on the Mkeka (mat) to symbolize the African concept of social parenting.

6. Zawadi (Sah-wah-dee) Gifts represent the fruits of the labor of the parents and are given as rewards and encouragement to the children to inspire them to continue to practice the values in the coming year.

7. Kikombe (Kee-coam-bay) The Cup symbolizes unity, the foundation principle. It is used exclusively for the libations ceremony .

*Vibunzi is the plural spelling for Kibunzi

KWANZAA CEREMONIAL ACTIVITIES

These ceremonies educate us in the richness of our heritage and remind us of the blessings our children bring, the work our elders have done for us and the task ahead of us.

GIVING THE LIBATION

Before the Libation is performed, a "Tamshi la tambiko" (libation statement/toast) is made honoring, praising and committing our people to the historical task begun by our ancestors. The libation (water, juice, wine) is poured from the Kikombe (cup) onto the floor in the direction of the four winds–north, south, east, west- in remembrance of the ancestors. Afterwards, each member of the immediate or extended family drinks from the Kikombe (cup).

THE GREETING

During KWANZAA, we greet each other by saying "Habari gani" (hah-BAH-ree-GAH-nee), which means "What's new?" The response should be whatever principle/day it is. For example, the first day the greeting would be "Habari Gani" and the response would be "Umoja," and on the second day the response would be "KUJICHAGULIA," and so on.

THE HARAMBEE

The Harambee is the call to Unity and Collective work and struggle. The Harambee call is always done in sets of seven to honor and reinforce the seven principles.

Harambee! Harambee! Harambee!
Harambee! Harambee!
Harambee! Harambee!

THE LIGHTING OF THE CANDLES

The lighting of the candles (mishumaa) is also a reinforcement of the seven principles. Each day during KWANZAA a candle is lit and the principle of that day is explained by the person lighting the candle; this is used as the main topic of discussion for that day. Any member may light the candles; however, it is suggested that children perform this activity as a way of teaching them the seven principles. There are seven candles–one black, three green and three red. The black candle is placed in the center; it represents unity, the first principle, and it is the first candle lit. The green candles are on the right side and the red candles are on the left and are lit from left to right alternately. Thus, the practice of lighting the red and then the green candles symbolizes that there must be struggle before a green future can be had.

On the second day, the first and second candles are lit; however, only the second principle is discussed that day and so forth. Finally, on the seventh day, all the candles are lit and the principle of Imani (faith) is discussed.

THE KARAMU (the Feast)
The KWANZAA Karamu feast is traditionally held on December 31st.

The Karamu is designated as a special time to celebrate Kwanzaa with the community. The celebration should be a cooperative as well as intergenerational affair shared by young and old together. When all ages celebrate together a bonding occurs and a greater sense of community develops among friends and families within neighborhoods and within organizations.

The place where the Karamu is held should also be decorated in the liberation colors of black, red and green. A large KWANZAA setting is also placed in the room of the Karamu, and a large Mkeka is placed in the center of the floor where all the food is placed for self-service. Before and during the feast, an informative and cultural program is presented. Traditionally, the program involves welcoming, remembering, reassessment and re-commitment and rejoicing, concluded by a farewell statement and call for greater unity.

The evening of Karamu is especially for adult partying and celebration; it is a time for fun, laughter, joy and high spirits.

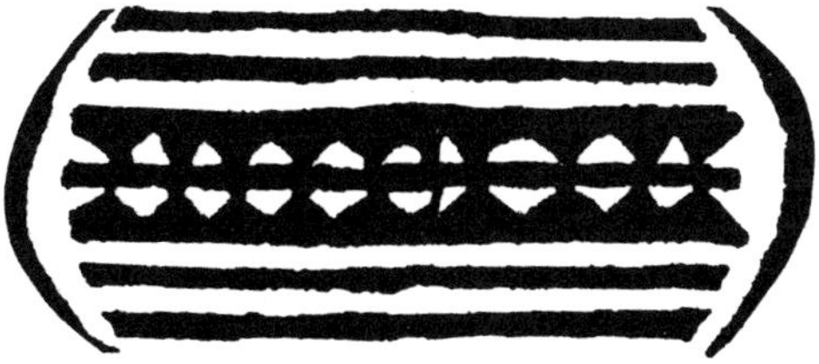

All KWANZAA principles, symbols, and ceremonies should be taken seriously and every attempt should be made to become familiar with the African words and pronunciation. Swahili is an easy and pleasant–sounding language, and it serves to remind us that there is more to us as a people than our experiences in America.

A WORD ABOUT GIFTS AND GIFT-GIVING

The last day of KWANZAA is IMANI (Faith). IMANI closes the holiday with quiet reflection on the coming year. The celebration of IMANI is also the time for gift-giving, especially from parents to children. Gifts should be given only to reward or encourage progress and/or achievement.

We parents, not the teachers, not the school system, not the churches or any other institution, are the first transmitters of cultural knowledge and information to our children. We must teach them that they have a heritage of greatness through hard work, honesty and high moral values to admire and to emulate. Our gifts, particularly during KWANZAA, should reflect and support these basic principles.

GIFT SUGGESTIONS

Video about famous Blacks
Books written by and about Blacks and Black experiences
Subscription to Black publications
Tickets to Black cultural events (plays, concerts, etc.)
Membership to African American Institutions (NAACP, African American Museum etc.)
Afrocentric Clothing
Products made by and for African Americans (afrocentric dolls, games etc.)

THE SCENE

"ONE OF THE GREATEST MEASURES OF A PEOPLE IS ITS CULTURE, ITS ARTISTIC STATURE".

PAUL ROBESON

THE AMBIENCE

KWANZAA can be celebrated in a number of ways, and as you and your family get comfortable with the rituals, you may wish to use your creativity and family wishes to expand on the procedures.

At minimum, a low table should be prepared in a prominent place in the home. The table should be covered with black or green material, and on that the Mkeka (mat) is placed. On the Mkeka (mat) the Kinara (candle holder) is placed. The *Vibunzi (ears of corn) should be placed around or on the side of the Kinara (candle holder), corresponding to the number of children the family has; if there are no children, at least one Kibunzi (ear of corn) should be placed to symbolize the concept of social parenthood. The Mazao (fruits and vegetables) should also be placed near the back of the Kinara (candle holder). The Unity cup (Kikombe) is placed in front of the Kinara.

The Mishumaa Saba (seven candles), which includes one black, three red and three green candles, are placed so that the black candle is in the center of the Kinara and the three red candles are on the left side and the three green candles are on the right. The gifts (Zawadi) may be placed toward the back of the KWANZAA setting on the last day.

*Vibunzi is the plural spelling for Kibunzi

KWANZAA PROTOCOL

One of the great thing about putting together a Kwanzaa Celebration is that it's a communal affair! You don't have to do all the work yourself. You do however, have to orchestrate everything. So, your job will be that of planning, organizing, reminding, and helping.

In organizing, you can loosely divide a Kwanzaa Celebration into four parts:

Part 1- Welcoming & Entertainment
Part 2- Ceremonies and Rituals
Part 3- Feasting
Part 4- Entertainment and Farewell

In general, each part will take approximately one hour, but there are no hard and fast rules on this–be flexible, go with the flow and the consensus of the group.

PART 1 - WELCOMING & ENTERTAINMENT

Guest should arrive to an atmosphere of gaiety and warmth. Music (African, jazz, rhythm & blues, gospel, etc.) can be playing in the background amidst the aromas of food, incense and oils.

The Greeters are responsible for welcoming guests in the African tradition and setting the tone for the evening (see Greeting, p.17). This will be a fun and interesting job and should be assigned to at least two people so that guests not familiar with the procedure can be given a demonstration.

It is a given that not everyone will arrive on time, so after a few guests have arrived, group singing should begin. Someone with a nice, strong voice should be assigned the job of leading the group in a few songs. Group singing always instills a feeling of unity and solidarity ; clapping, shouting, hand–holding can all be part of the celebration. (See Songs on p. 68). Other entertainment/cultural expression should follow (poetry reading, storytelling, drumming, skits, performances, etc.).
After light conversation and entertainment, the ceremonial rituals should begin.

PART 2 - CEREMONIES AND RITUALS

The ceremonial rituals are usually led by one of the elders or the head of the home. Everyone should gather around the Mkeka (mat) and Kinara (candle holder) in an atmosphere of reverence. Smoking, talking or other distractions should be prohibited.

There are two parts to this ceremony: "Spiritual Expression" and "Knowledge Transmission." The Spiritual Expression is very sacred and should be assigned to someone held in high esteem by the family or community. The person assigned to lead the Spiritual Expression is responsible for: (1) giving the "Tamshi la tambiko" (Libation Statement/ toast), (2) pouring of the libation, and (3) leading the Harambee. Knowledge Transmission is of equal importance and should also be assigned to someone who is well respected in the family or community. An outstanding young person may also assist in this part of the ceremony.

The person(s) assigned to lead the Knowledge Transmission are responsible for: (1) lighting the candle(s), (2) stating the principle for the day, (3) giving the lesson of the day, and (4) leading the group discussion.

The ceremony begins with a "Tamshi la tambiko" (libation statement/ toast). See page 72 for sample. The Kikombe (cup) is used to pour the libation, which can be water, juice or any liquid agreed upon by the group. The libation is poured on the floor in four directions (east, west, north, and south). It is not necessary to drench the floor–a few drops are sufficient to symbolize the connection between ourselves and our ancestors and clears the way for the rest of the ceremony.

The person giving the libation holds the Kikombe (cup) with both hands and drinks from the Kikombe (cup), and then leads the group in a call to unity by shouting "Harambee" seven times. After the collective Harambee, the Kikombe (cup) is passed around to the elders first and then to the others. For large groups, paper cups may be substituted.

The next part of the ceremony is Knowledge Transmission. Children are especially encouraged to be involved in this part of the ceremony, for it is they who will carry on the work and the ritual after we are gone. A good way might be for the children to light the candle and recite the principle for the day and its meaning. An adult can then further explain the principle for the day and share examples of heroic Blacks who exemplify the principle (Harriet Tubman, Booker T. Washington, Mary Bethune, etc.). The discussion should then be opened for others to recount what they have done during the year to live up to the principle, and what they pledge to do for the coming year.

This ends the most formal and ceremonial part of the celebration.

PART 3 - FEASTING

Next, the feast begins, but before food is made available, "Thanks" should be given for the blessing of the past year (new births, family, friends, food about to be received, etc.). This can be done through prayer or in silent meditation. The food is passed to the elders first and then to the others.

PART 4 - ENTERTAINMENT AND FAREWELL

After the meal, guests should be entertained through cultural expressions, music, dance etc.

The evening's events should be completed with a Farewell Statement from an elder or the head of the home. See sample Farewell Statement on page 72.

By now you've probably noticed that there is a certain theme that runs throughout the Kwanzaa Celebration, which is: **LIVE, LOVE, LEARN AND LEAVE LEGACY.**

In keeping with that theme, here's a wonderful supporting activity that everyone can participate in, including children. As your guests arrive, have the greeters give each person a slip of paper. Have each guest write down what he or she has learned or wants to share about life and living with the group (papers can be signed or unsigned). It could be a positive thought, an instructive observation or words of wisdom. The responses should be folded up and placed in a container before the meal is served. After everyone has eaten, the host or someone of his/her choosing should read each of the responses to the group.

These will be wonderful memorabilia to keep and treasure as the years progress. You and your children will look back and remember that funny saying Uncle Ben wrote or that very wise thought aunt Mamie gave.

PREPARATION

"TO MAKE PREPARATION DOES NOT SPOIL THE TRIP".

GUINEA PROVERB

getting started........

It is very important that planning and preparation be done well ahead of time. The celebration should go as smoothly and as calmly as possible so that it becomes an activity that the whole family can look forward to each year. You may also have guests who have never before attended a KWANZZA ceremony, so it is important to remember that you are a role model and teacher for your guests and also for the children who will pass on the legacy to their children.

Here we have created a four–step planning schedule so you will have plenty of time to complete everything in a relaxed and peaceful manner.

STAGE 1- SIX WEEKS BEFORE KWANZAA

- Make guest list.
- Make and send invitations or call folks
- Get commitments from everyone who will participate in program (greeters, etc.).

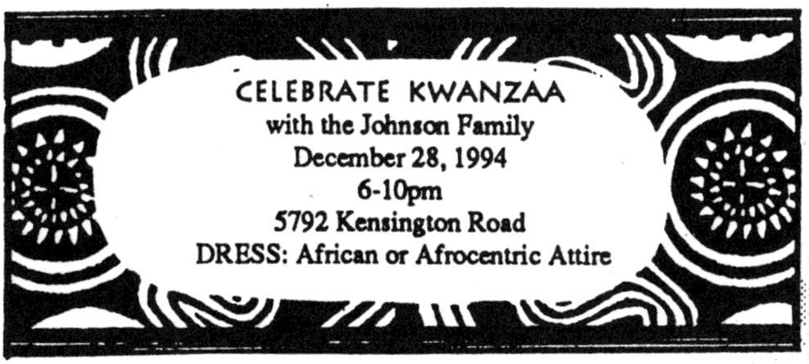

- Obtain food and drink commitments from guests. Tradition calls for Soul, Southern or African foods, but it is also important to be health smart. High blood pressure, high cholesterol and obesity are prevalent in our communities. We should plan and prepare foods with this in mind.

- Get commitment from someone to arrange for music (taped and/or live) and other entertainment (African dancers, story-tellers, performers, etc.)

STAGE 2-FOUR WEEKS BEFORE KWANZAA

- Collect/make decorations (banners, flags, streamers, etc.).

- Collect items you will need for the ceremonies. "The Complete Kwanzaa Celebration Basket" will have most of what you need (see order form in back).

- Write role of all participants on 3x5 cards and give to them (greeters, persons to do prayer, libation, unity call, farewell statement etc.).

> Lead Farewell Statement
> Rev. Phyllis Johnston
>
> Role: To give Farewell Statement
>
> Procedure: On word from host, gather group together in a circle; hold hands and give a farewell statement.

> Greeter: Jina McDougal
>
> Role :To welcome all guests coming to Kwanzaa celebration.
> Procedure: As each guest comes in say to them:
> "HABARI GANI?"
> (HAH-BAH-REE-GAH-NEE)
> which means "What's New?" The response from them should be the principle for that day.
> For example: on the first day of Kwanzaa, the greeting "HABARI GANI?" should bring the response "UMOJA," on the second day when the greeting is said, the response should be " KUJICHAGULIA"
> Guests not familiar with this should be given a demonstration until they catch on.

- Collect the things you will need for children's games and activities.

STAGE 3- TWO WEEKS BEFORE KWANZAA

- Decorate home.
- Make a program booklet.
- Confirm program participants, people bringing food and beverage, and all entertainment.
- Assign someone to take pictures.
- Schedule a day before KWANZAA for children to draw, make jewelry, clothing etc. to wear/display at KWANZAA.

STAGE 4 - THE DAY BEFORE KWANZAA

- Prepare food.
- Rearrange room (if needed) for easy seating.
- Put away any unusual or expensive items (antiques, breakables).
- Have extra trash bags ready for disposable items.

THE PROGRAM BOOKLET

Another idea for keeping the ceremony organized and flowing smoothly is to do a Program Booklet. It doesn't takes much time to do, but its one of those little added touches that will be very meaningful in later years. See example on page 66 .

A Program Booklet can serve several purposes:

- It can be used as as invitations to invite guests to the celebration. Note: KWANZAA is an excellent time to invite in neighbors and acquaintances who may not have anyone to share the holidays with (singles, seniors, etc.).

- It lets everyone know who does what and when. Also, when people see their name in print they tend to take the activity and their role more seriously.
- The Program booklet serves as a memento/remebrance of the celebration.

- Program booklets along with pictures, can be used creatively as decorations for the next year's celebrations. This is a great activity to have the young people do.

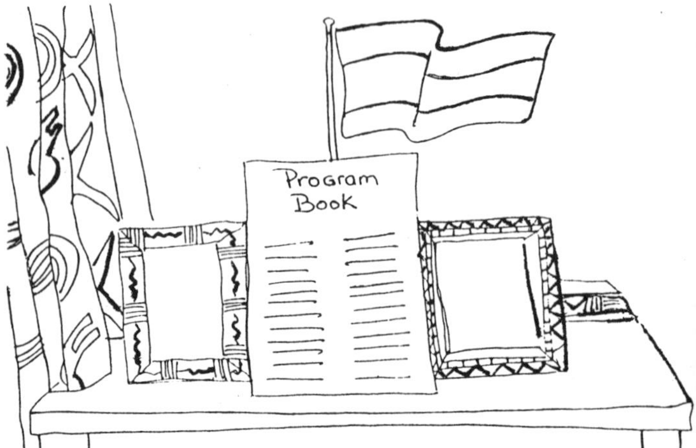

SOME FINAL DO'S & DON'TS

Do........

Be flexible!!!!!

Be clear about the time the program will start.

Make it easy for people to wait on themselves.

Ask older children to help with the younger children.

Include yourself in the fun and festivities.

Don't........

Overdo.

Spend a lot of money on unnecessary things.

KWANZAA & CHILDREN

"IT IS THE RESPONSIBILITY OF EVERY ADULT - ESPECIALLY PARENTS, EDUCATORS AND RELIGIOUS LEADERS - TO MAKE SURE THAT CHILDREN HEAR WHAT WE HAVE LEARNED FROM THE LESSONS OF LIFE AND TO HEAR OVER AND OVER THAT WE LOVE THEM AND THAT THEY ARE NOT ALONE."

MARIAN WRIGHT EDELMAN

CHILDREN'S ACTIVITIES

The traditions and ceremonies of KWANZAA give us an excellent way of transmitting positive cultural values to our children. Therefore, it is important that children be involved in the ceremony as much as possible, and that activities are created to help them learn the principles in a joyful way.

Below are a few games to start you thinking about ways children can be involved in the preparation, the ceremony, and after–holiday celebration of KWANZAA.

GAME
WHO AM I ?

On 3x5 cards write down the definition of each of the seven principles and the symbols of KWANZAA.

Pass them out to the children during the planning & preparation phase and have each child memorize one principle and/or one symbol of KWANZAA.

On each night of KWANZAA have a few children enact the principle they have learned and ask those in attendance to guess what the principle is.

Examples:

A child says, "I strive for and maintain oneness in my family, community, nation and race." Who am I ?

Another child says, "We build and maintain our own stores, shops and other businesses and we profit from them together." Who am I?

Another child says "I am the original stalk from which we all sprang." Who am I ?

This should be very lively, entertaining and instructive for both children and adults. Once all the children have presented, the presentations should conclude with seven Harambees.

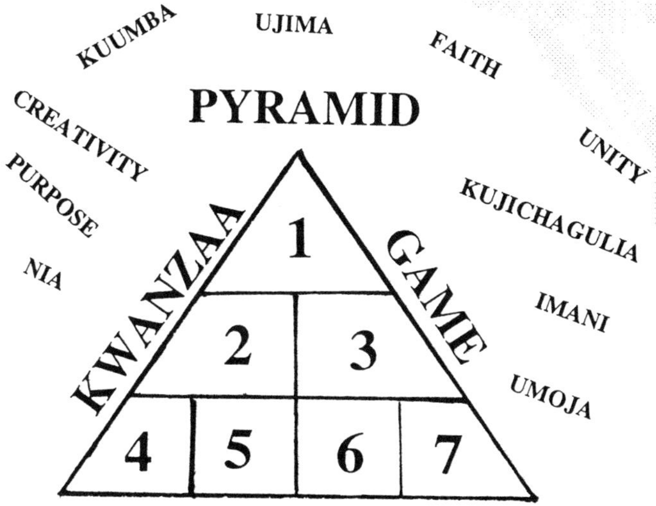

Draw a large pyramid on a poster board (see illustration) and divide into three rows: four columns on the lower row, two columns on the middle row, and one at the top.

On 3x5 cards write the seven principles in English and again in Swahili, and mix them up.

Have children match the African words with the American words (make sure to have them pronounce the African words).

Put the seven principle in order.

Fill in the correct principle on the pyramid.

Talk about how the seven principles are related.

OUR FAMILY KWANZAA BOOK

Have children write story/draw pictures about the KWANZAA celebration at their house.

This is me drawing about the seven nights of Kwanzaa and the seven principles

By Andre Elston
age 9
school Bates academy

Outfits you can wear to Kwanzaa celebrations.

THINGS CHILDREN CAN MAKE FOR KWANZAA

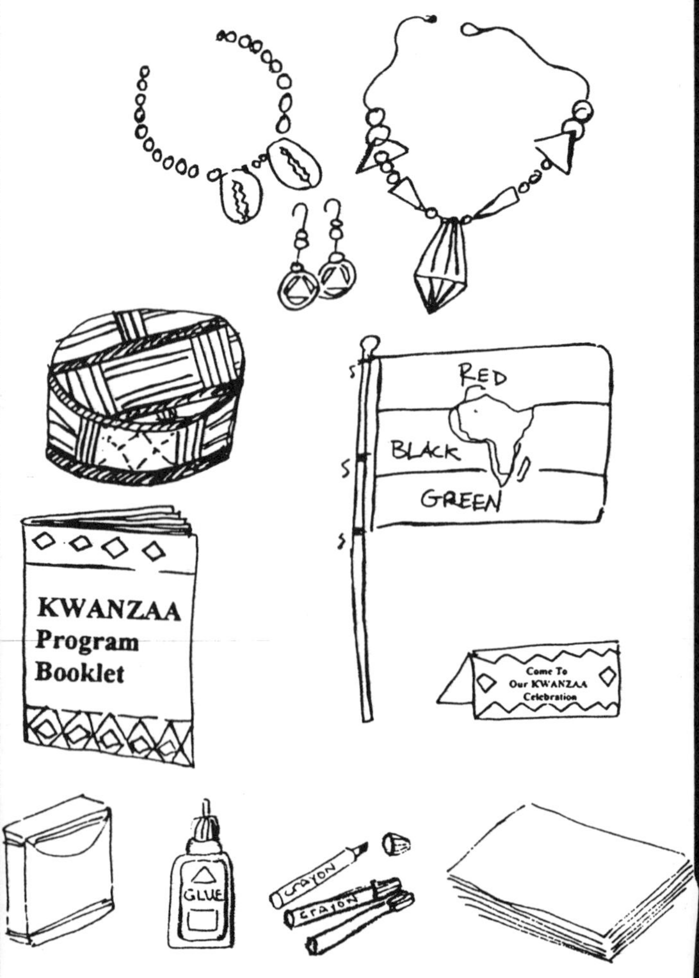

KWANZAA YEAR-ROUND

"EDUCATION IS YOUR PASSPORT TO THE FUTURE, FOR TOMORROW BELONGS TO THE PEOPLE WHO PREPARE FOR IT TODAY"

MALCOLM X
EL-HAJJ MALIK EL SHABAZZ

KWANZAA YEAR-ROUND ACTIVITIES

The Seven Principles of Kwanzaa form the basis of a self-help program for African Americans. It gives us a blueprint to achieve personal excellence and it teaches us how to improve ourselves within the context of our culture, thereby improving the moral, physical and spiritual condition of our people.

The principles are to be incorporated into our daily lives and practiced throughout the year. You and your family may wish to focus on one principle each month (January through July) and then work on activities that combine the principles for the remainder of the year. Or you may wish to focus on one principle per day. For example, every Monday you and your family could focus on Unity (Umoja), every Tuesday, Self-determination (Kujichagulia) and so on. It doesn't matter what method you use to practice the principles as long as you're consistent. At the end of the year, December 26th through January 1st, we then come together with family and friends to share and celebrate our growth in becoming and living a life centered in principle.

In the spirit of Unity and Collective Work we have solicited suggestions and ideas from a broad range of people on ways you can incorporate the seven principle into your lifestyle. The suggestions and ideas reflect our collective outpouring of love to you as well as our wish for you to live life at the highest level of human existence (physical, spiritual and cultural).
Most of the suggestion are activities that can be done easily by anyone, with little or no money. We invite you to adopt the ones that make sense for you and your family.

To complete the circle of collective teaching and learning, we invite you to share your ideas with us in the revised publication of The Complete Kwanzaa Celebration Book. Send suggestions to the address on the back.

UMOJA (UNITY)

First establish unity within yourself, making sure that your body, mind and spirit are consistent with the things you want to achieve.

For example:

GOAL ↓	UNITY IN		
	Mind	Body	Spirit
Good health	Think positive thoughts	Exercise & eat healthy foods	Mediate & Pray
More love in your life	Love self	Be open to others	Love GOD

⌘

Look into a mirror and affirm daily: I work to enhance both my inner and outer world. I think positive thoughts, I take positive action and contribute to the well-being of my world and all that is within my world. I willingly and enthusiastically live in harmony with others.

⌘

Create/engage in intergenerational family activities (things that people of all age groups can participate in), watch video and TV together, and go on family outings, picnics, trips to African American museums and historic sites. Minimize children going in one direction and adults going another.

⌘

Have regular rap sessions with your family or group to build and strengthen bonds of communication, trust and support for example, once a week for 1/2 hour- 1 hour. Here are some exercises to try with your family:
Have each member tell each of the other family members what positive quality or behavior he or she demonstrated in the past week that you admired. For example, Daughter talking to Brother, Mom and Dad could say: "Jason, the positive behavior that you demonstrated last week that I

admired was self control. When those boys down the street started cursing at you, you politely told them off and walked away." "Mom, the positive quality that you demonstrated last week that I admired was listening. You listened to why I skipped school last Tuesday without judging or blaming me." "Dad the positive quality that you demonstrated last week that I admired was persistence. Even though you didn't get that job that you wanted, you didn't give up. You got a part time job until you find something better."

⌘

Have each member tell what he or she did during the pass week that they felt good about, and (2) what they plan to work on/focus on for the next week. The idea here is to praise people for their accomplishments and to support them in their challenges for the upcoming week. For example, Daughter might say, "I felt good about getting a "B" on my English test. Last time my grad was "D". This week I am going to work on getting my room organized." Mom might say, "I felt good about paying off the bill for our furniture. This week I'm going to work on spending some quality time with myself (doing something nice for me)." Son might say, "I felt really good about my date with Kisha last week. This week I'm going to work on getting a summer job at one of the fast food restaurants in the neighborhood."

⌘

Have family meetings (example: monthly for 1 1/2 - 2 hours) to create family goals and action plans. Vote on things the family wants to accomplish, and give time lines and role and responsibilities for who does what.

⌘

Establish a monthly UMOJA award and give it to the family member who best promotes unity in the family or community.

⌘

Agree as a family to "Adopt a Value" or attribute that will be observed by all to make the family a stronger unit. For example, agree to refrain from the use of profanity in the presence of elders and children.

⌘

Regularly tell those you love that you do. Openly express affection for one another.

⌘

Agree to have dinner together as a family at least twice a week (example: Wednesdays & Sundays).

⌘

Agree that everyone will support each other in their outside pursuits. Attend games, performances, recognition's of other family members.

⌘

Have family dress up in their African attire and go out and spend the evening together.

⌘

Agree that each family member will explore the life of one of their ancestors and share the information gathered during monthly meetings. The culmination of this activity will produce a collection of your heritage to be shared with future generations. Each participant should also prepare a self-portrait that will be added to the collection.

KUJICHAGULIA
(SELF DETERMINATION)

Affirm each day: I have the time, ability, energy and determination to do all that is before me to do. I move easily and with sureness of purpose.

⌘

Agree to establish a monthly Kujichagulia award and give it to the family member who demonstrates the highest degree of self-discipline and/or self-determination such as:

> Completing job/task before doing what you want to do (work before play), for example,cleaning up your room before going out to play basketball.
>
> Doing work you know you should do before you are told, for example, taking out thegarbage before you are reminded because it's your job, or you notice it's full or smelling.

⌘

Have adolescents (ages 11-17) interview senior relatives and family friends, collecting interesting stories of challenges faced and overcome, tales of life-affirming or humorous experiences. (example: How and when did the family migrate from the South to the North, or from East to West). These stories could be shared at family gatherings or become bedtime stories for the youngest members of the clan. Collected stories might be memorized or written down. An album of specially selected family photos could be used to tell the tale.

⌘

Locate or make a calendar that gives the events and dates relevant to the Black struggle for self-determination. Place calendar where it can be viewed the by entire family.
For example:
1935- The National Council of Negro Women was established by Mary McLeod Bethune in Washington D.C.
1955- The Montgomery bus boycott began as a result of Rosa Park's refusal to ride in the back of the bus.

⌘

Read motivational literature (books, tapes, etc.). Attend self-improvement seminars. Study hard.

⌘

Agree that once a month the family/group will pool money to rent or purchase videos about an African American who overcame against the odds.

⌘

Research African heritage. Determine countries African Americans most likely came from, or pick an African country you'd like to know more about. Identify the capital city, products they export, the country's natural resources, when independence occurred, etc. Also learn about the difference tribes within the country, their customs, language, etc.

⌘

Give each family member an African name and together research the name and meaning.

⌘

Pick a career or profession that interest you and start collecting books, articles, photos, videos, etc., of famous, successful or notable African Americans in that field.
For example: In the field of Medical Surgery–
Follow the career of Alexa Canady, the first African American neurosurgeon in the U.S.
Read *Think Big* and *Gifted Hands*, the autobiography of Dr. Ben S. Carson, Director of Pediatric Neurosurgery at Johns Hopkins University.

⌘

UJIMA (COLLECTIVE WORK AND RESPONSIBILITY)

Affirm daily: I reach out to others with positive expectation. Good is accomplished through my work and the work of others.

⌘

Agree on roles and responsibilities of family/group members. For example, adult's responsibilities could include:

providing food, clothing and shelter;
protecting from harm and danger;
teaching values and
loving unconditionally.

children's responsibilities could include:

obedience to parents & elders;
care of own possessions (toys, games, cloths, school supplies) and
completing daily and weekly chores.

⌘

Agree to establish monthly Ujimaa award and give it to the member who best demonstrates the principle.

⌘

Start a business or entrepreneurial venture.

⌘

Organize and participate in the cleanup and maintenance of vacant property in your community.

⌘

Once a month, or at regular intervals, agree to fix a family meal together. Each person should have responsibility for some portion of the meal (bread, salad, grains, vegetables, meat if used, dessert, drinks, etc.) Each member should tell why he or she selected that particular food (taste, variety, cost, etc.) and the benefits the family will derive from it (high in Vitamin C, builds strong bones etc.).

⌘

Organize neighborhood youth to do chores for the elderly and disabled in the neighborhood (rake leaves, shovel snow, pick up paper on the street, run errands, etc.). Stress the privilege of helping and serving others.

⌘

Have each family member agree to foster, mentor or take care of a younger person (sibling, friend of family, relative, neighbor) or pet for a specific period of time (example: one month). Help with homework, read a story, teach something (how to grow tomatoes, how to iron own clothes, etc.) Discuss the privilege of helping and serving others.

⌘

Organize a "Rite of Passage" program for girls and boys at church and/or in your community. Good books to help you get started are: *Bringing The Black Boy Into Manhood; the passage* by Drs. Nathan and Julia Hare; The Black Think Tank Press, San Francisco, CA. and *Transformation: A Rites of Passage Manual for African American Girls*, by Moore, Gilyard, King and Warfield-Coppock, Star Press, New York, NY.

⌘

Organize a "Books for Babies" program by bringing together community groups to donate children's books to disadvantage teen mothers so that they have positive Afrocentric stories to read to their babies.

⌘

Join and contribute to local and national organizations that work for the health, education and well-being of African Americans.

⌘

UJAMAA
(COOPERATIVE ECONOMICS)

Affirm daily: I cooperate with others, I prepare myself for financial exchanges with others and anticipate positive outcomes to every situation. I use my talents in cooperation with the talents of others and together we prosper.

⌘

Start a business or entrepreneurial venture.

⌘

Pool money together as a family and start an investment club.

⌘

Send money or a child to a Black college.

⌘

Have family members agree to spend money at African American businesses and establishments. Save receipts and give the monthly Ujamaa award to the family member who presents the most receipts from African American establishments.

example:

UJAMAA Award
to
Ebony Simpkins
Month of August 1994
for Patronizing African American
Bookstore & Cleaners

⌘

Organize and/or participate in community scholarship fund raiser. This could become an annual event.

⌘

Open up savings and checking accounts at a Black bank and deposit money regularly.

⌘

Organize a jewelry club for teen-age girls (11-16). Shop for wholesale beads and discuss the advantages of quantity/

discount purchases. When necklaces, earrings, bracelets etc. are completed, culminate the activity with a jewelry party for the community. Use money to purchase more beads.

⌘

Promote the talents, businesses and entrepreneurial ventures of your friends and family (tell others about what they do).

⌘

Begin family "Save Up Program". Make a game or activity out of looking for the best deals on items the family has agreed to purchase. Read about best brand (Consumer Reports, etc.) and set goals as to when you should buy it. Talk about the discipline of planning, saving and waiting to reap the best reward.

For example:

Family goal → to purchase new TV in 6 months

Family responsibilities	family member	financial commitment	time/resources commitment
	Dad	$100 per month	collect money each month
	Mom	$100 per month	plan day to do comparison shopping
	teen	$20 per month	read consumer magazine on best brands
	youth	$5.00 per month	work with brother and write top three choices

⌘

Hire African Americans from your neighborhood, fraternity, sorority, club, etc., to perform services and jobs for you. (ex. doctors, dentists, plumbers, electricians, insurance agents etc.).

⌘

NIA (PURPOSE)

Affirm daily: I have a special contribution to make to life, and I do so freely and joyfully. My purpose and place are made clear as I pray, receive guidance and take positive action.

⌘

Agree that each family member will set short-term goals (things that can be achieved within one year) and long-term goals (things that will take several years to achieve). Agree that everyone will share goals with the entire family. Agree that family members will help/support each other in the attainment of each other's goals.

⌘

Agree that every family member will make a list of his or her talents (things that they are good at and enjoy doing). The list should include everything they can think of: skills, aptitude, and attitude (good tennis player, good debater, good listener, good at computer games, etc.). Share the list with family members and have them add to the list the things they think you're talented in. Practice recognizing and identifying your own talents and the talents of others.

⌘

Accept responsibility for developing your own individual talents. At least once a week do something to strengthen and develop one of your many talents.

⌘

Create a "Family Creed". Have each family member nominate at least four words you want your family to stand for (honesty, integrity, love, loyalty, etc.). Discuss their importance. Each person has three votes. Make up a chart showing the three winning words. Display it where everyone can see.

⌘

Talk about the talents of famous people and discuss how they used their talents to express their purpose. For example, some of Dr. Martin Luther King's talents that he strengthened and improved were:

1. Speaking
2. Leadership

He developed his speaking talent and became a great orator/speaker.

He developed his leadership talent and brought people together.

After he worked on and developed these talents he used them to realize his purpose, to lead the greatest civil /human rights movement in the history of the United States.

⌘

Establish a monthly NIA award and give to the person who has shown great progress in developing his or her talents.

⌘

Agree as a family to give gifts that would help strengthen the talents of individual family members. For example, give a year's worth of lessons (dance, piano, flying, etc.); instruments (musical, scientific); supplies and equipment (paints, easels, etc.) and "How To" books.

⌘

Study and learn about the history of Black people.

⌘

Issue a community flyer that presents information about the positive contributions of community residents as well as other local news that highlight the accomplishment of Black people in your neighborhood.

⌘

KUUMBA (CREATIVITY)

Affirm daily: I free myself to experience new ideas, new awareness, new understandings. My thoughts are charged with positive energy and I go forth to create grace and beauty in my world.

⌘

Start an "Adopt a Grandparent" program in your community.

⌘

Establish a monthly Kuumba award and give it to family member who has used his or her creativity to enhance the cultural expression or the cultural knowledge of the group. example:

Atiba Anderson
Kuumba Award
May 1994
for star performance
in *A Raisin in the Sun.*

⌘

Think of ways to beautify your home using natural materials. Start a beautification contest in the neighborhood.

⌘

Buy African American collectibles (Black culture). Black dolls, baseball cards, movies, figurines, art, etc.).

⌘

Display Black culture in your home.

⌘

Make your own cards and gifts for family and friends.

⌘

Learn to cook African and Caribbean foods (fu fu, red beans and rice, etc.) and listen to African and Caribbean music (reggae, high life, etc.)

⌘

Through the local community center or neighborhood association, sponsor art, music, poetry and craft fairs. This could include a "Mental Olympics" for all ages: checkers, chess, cards, dominoes, horseshoes, etc.

⌘

Make plaques, T-shirts, hats etc. with family creed and or family prayer on it. Wear at special family functions.

⌘

Expose family/group to a variety of cultural activities (museums, concerts, festivals, art fairs etc.) Talk and learn about the cultures of other ethnic groups.

⌘

Teach children to take care of the earth by planting flowers and vegetables and caring for yards and gardens. This activity will also add to the beauty of your home and neighborhood.

⌘

Dream freely, envision excellence, excude enthusiam, be inspired, inspire others, take pride in you, laugh often, recognize inner beauty, draw on inner strength, look inside your soul, create peace, seek truth, spread joy, embark on adventure, live fully, reach out, aim high, find happiness, expect the best.

⌘

IMANI (FAITH)

Affirm daily: I have unshakable and invincible faith in GOD, and in his Goodness. Fear of the unknown, concerns about the future, and regrets about the past are all swept away. I meet each day with active faith and give thanks for both expected and unexpected good.

⌘

Read inspirational literature.

⌘

Create your own family prayer and recite together at dinner and special family functions.

⌘

Create your own family affirmation and recite daily.

⌘

Affirm collectivism as it pertains to the upliftment of the group. For those who pray, pray for the group. For those who strive for success, wealth and recognition for themselves, also strive for power, dignity, and integrity for the group.

⌘

Establish a monthly Imani award and give to the family member who best demonstrates faith in GOD, self and/or other family members.

⌘

Make a special point to tell an African American youth that you have faith in his or her ability to make correct choices, and that you have faith that they will accomplish their goals.

⌘

Worship together as a family and attend other religious functions and activities (gospel concerts, revivals prayer meetings etc.).

⌘

Take a chance, take a risk. Do something that requires a leap of faith in self or in GOD. Learn and grow from all outcomes you experience.

⌘

Remember that faith overcomes fear (the major factor that holds us back from realizing the fullness of ourselves). Keep the faith.

⌘

CONTRIBUTORS

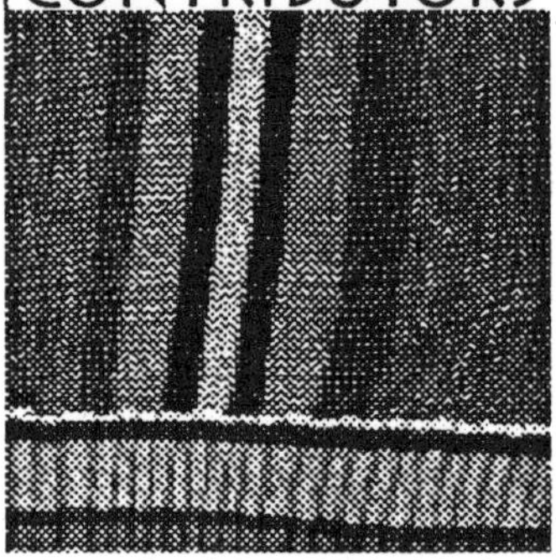

DR. SHARRON HELM
KEITH WHITE
ANTHONY BERNARD
GLORIA JEAN VANCE
SHARON KEENER
EILEENE GORDON-KING
MINNIE PHILLIPS
RITA MATTHEWS
CARL S. PAYNE
STUDENTS AND STAFF AT THE MARCUS GARVEY ACADEMY IN DETROIT
DANNY BROWN
N'GERE ABDUL WALI
RUTHIE WHITE
ANTONETTA JOHNSON-GARDNER
LONA LOMAN
VIVIAN GIBSON
KEVIN TAYLOR

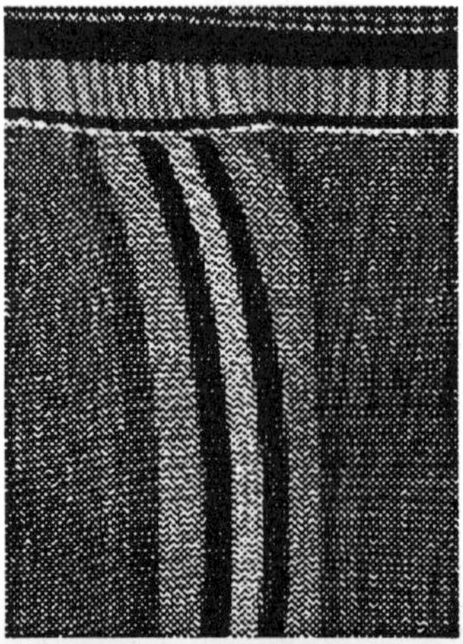

APPENDIX

"HERE NOW IN OUR SWIFTLY PACED TECHNOLOGICAL ERA, IT SEEMS TO ME THAT NOT ONLY YOUNGER BLACK PEOPLE, BUT WE OLDER ONES AS WELL, NEED URGENTLY TO SHOW OUR LIVING GRANDPARENTS' GENERATION THAT WE DO REALIZE AND RESPECT AND HONOR HOW MUCH WE HAVE INHERITED AND BENEFITED BECAUSE OF THE EXPERIENCES WHICH THEY SURVIVED."

ALEX HALEY

Here is a suggested model program for the Karamu feast.

KWANZAA KARAMU

Welcoming
a. Introductory Remarks
b. Recognition of Distinguished Guests
c. Cultural Expression

Remembering
a. Reflection of a Man
b. Reflection of a Woman
c. Reflection of a Youth
d. Cultural Expression

Reassessment and Recommitment
a. Introduction of Distinguished Guest Lecturer
b. Guest Lecturer Topic

Rejoicing
Karamu Feast
a. Libation Statement
b. Unity Cup
c. Cultural Expression

Farewell Statement

KWANZAA CELEBRATION

Program Book
199_
DAY ONE

HOME OF______________________________

LOCATION____________________________

WELCOME
GREETERS(adult)______________________________

(child)______________________________

CULTURAL EXPRESSION
a. Group Songs led by Wendell Morton
b. Poetry read by Wilma Roberts
c. Video - The Life of Paul Robeson

SPIRITUAL EXPRESSION
Led by Elder James Johnson
a. Toast
b. Libation
c. Call to Unity

KNOWLEDGE TRANSMISSION

a. Explanation of Principle for day
George Smith Jr.
b. Lighting of the candle(s)
George Smith Jr.
c. Historical Lesson - Sister Carry Smith
d. Group discussion and pledges for the new year - led by Sister Carry Smith

FEAST

a. Prayer led by Sister Deborah Payne

b. Food prepared by Lucille Wells, Barbara Miller, Shirley Jackson, Mozella Garrett, Vina Price, Jerry Barker, Tisanda Wells, Monique Hall, and Ben Coleman

ENTERTAINMENT/CULTURAL EXPRESSION

a. Play: "Who Am I?" performed by Tisanda Wells, Monique Hall, Patrick Hall, Kevin Davis

b. Musical Selection by Kenya Payne

c. Musical Selection by "The Grove"

FAREWELL STATEMENT- Rev. Phyllis Johnston

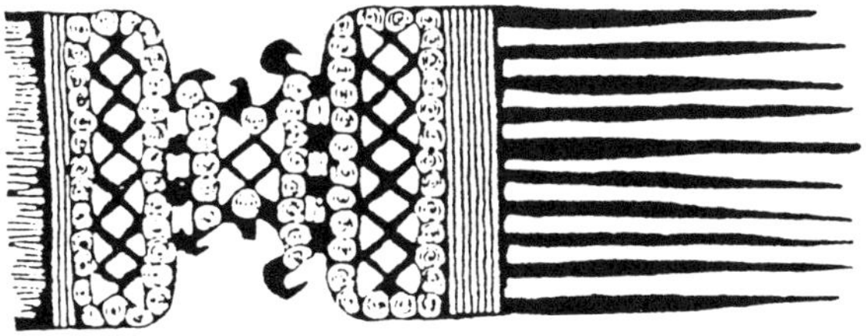

We Shall Overcome

New words and arrangement by Zilphia Horton,
Frank Hamilton, Guy Carawan, and Pete Seeger

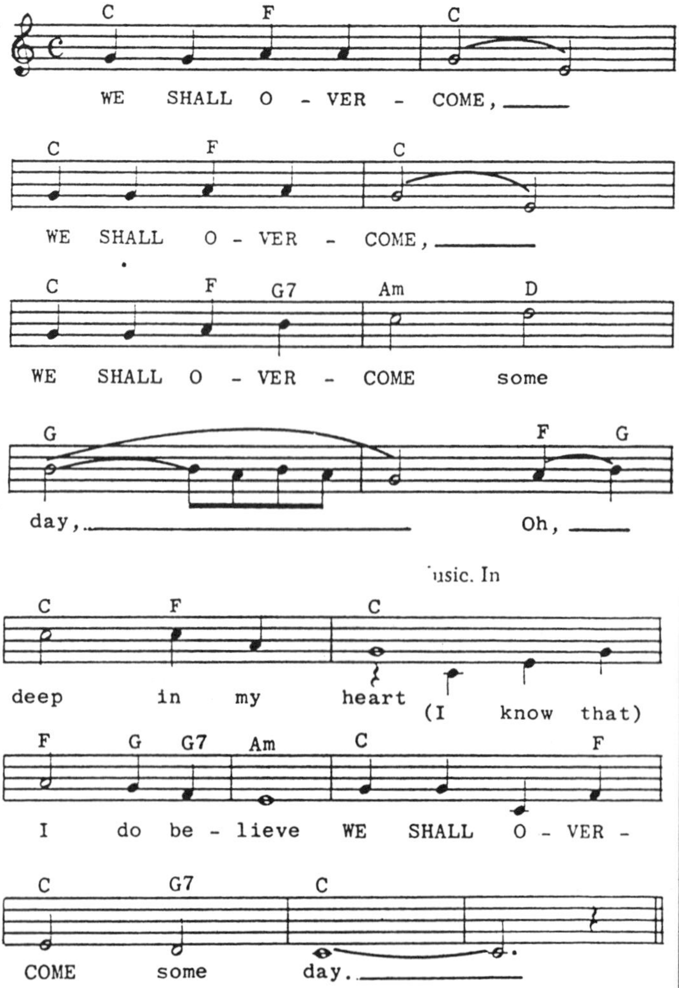

2. We'll walk hand in hand, we'll walk hand in hand,
We'll walk hand in hand, some day.
Oh, deep in my heart I do believe,
That we shall overcome some day.

3. We are not afraid, we are not afraid,
We are not afraid, today.
Oh, deep in my heart I do believe,
That we shall overcome some day.

4. We shall live in peace, we shall live in peace,
We shall live in peace, so day.
Oh, deep in my heart I do believe,
That we shall overcome some day.

(Additional verses)

We are not alone, etc.

The Lord will see us through, etc.

The truth will make us free, etc.

We shall brothers be, etc.

Keep Your Eyes on the Prize

Paul and Silas begin to shout,
The jail door opened and they
walked on out.
Keep your eyes on the prize, hold on.

Freedom's name is mighty sweet,
Soon one day we're gonna meet,
Keep your eyes on the prize, hold on.

Got my hand on the Gospel plow,
I wouldn't take nothing for my
journey now.
Keep your eyes on the prize, hold on.

The only chain that a man can stand,
Is the chain of hand in hand.
Keep your eyes on the prize, hold on.

The only thing that we did wrong,
Stayed in the wilderness a day too
long.
Keep your eyes on the prize, hold on.

But the one thing we did right,
Was the day we started to fight.
Keep your eyes on the prize, hold on.

We're gonna board that big Greyhound
Carryin' love from town to town.
Keep your eyes on the prize, hold on.

We're gonna ride for civil rights,
We're gonna ride for black and whites.
Keep your eyes on the prize, hold on.

We've met jail and violence too,
But God's love has seen us through.
Keep your eye on the prize, hold on.

Haven't been to heaven but I've been told,
Streets up there are paved with gold.
Keep your eyes on the prize, hold on.

A LIBATION STATEMENT
(Tamshi La Tambiko)

For Africa, the motherland, cradle of civilization .
For our ancestors and their courageous spirit.
For our elders who sacrified much for us.
For our youth, who represent our hope for tomorrow and tomorrow's tomorrow.
For our people, the original people.
For the righteous struggle of Black people aroung the world.
For Umoja, the principle of unity which should guide us in all that we do.
For the creator who provides all things great and small.

THE FAREWELL STATEMENT

Strive for discipline, dedication and achievement in all you do. Struggle and sacrifice and gain the strength that comes from this. Build where you are and leave a legacy that will last as long as the sun shines and the waters flow. Practice daily the Seven Principles: Umoja, Kujichagulia, Ujima, Ujamaa, Nia, Kuumba and Imani. And may the wisdom of the ancestors always walk with us. May the year's end meet us laughing and stronger. May our children honor us by following our example in love and struggle. And at the end of the year, may we sit again together, in larger numbers, with greater achievement and closer to liberation and a higher level of human life.

HARAMBEE! HARAMBEE! HARAMBEE!

HARAMBEE! HARAMBEE! HARAMBEE!
HARAMBEE!

BIBLIOGRAPHY

Primary source
"KWANZAA: Origin, Concepts, Practice," by Dr. Maulana Karenga, Kwaida Publications, Los Angeles, California (1977).

"Kwanzaa: A Progressive and Uplifting African American Holiday," by Haki R. Madhubuti, Third World Press, Chicago, Illinois (1972).

"Kwanza: Everything You Always Wanted to Know But Didn't Know Where to Ask" by Cedric McClester, Gumbs & Thomas, Publishers, Inc. (1990).

Secondary Sources
"KWANZAA: An Everyday Resource and Instructional Guide," by David A. Anderson, Gumbs & Thomas, Publishers, Inc., New York, NY (1990).

"First Fruit: A Family Guide for Celebrating KWANZAA," by Imani Abegunde Humphrey, Affirmative Learning Services, Highland Park, Michigan (1982).

"How to Celebrate KWANZAA," Detroit Black Writers Guild, Detroit, Michigan, 1988.

INDEX

Adopt A Grand Parent
  Program, 59
Adopt A Value, 49
Ambience, 23
Bethune, Mary McLeod, 51
Books for Baby Program, 54
Canady, Alexa, 52
Candles, 15, 18, 23
Carson, Ben S., 52
Checklist, 31
Ceremonies, 24, 25
  Knowledge transmission, 26
  spiritual expression, 25
Children Activities, 39, 44
Collective Work &
  Responsibility, 18
  definition, 13
  activities, 53
Cooperative Economics
  definition, 14
  activities, 55
Creativity
  definition, 14
  activities, 59
Do's and Don'ts, 35
Entertainment, 24, 27
Faith
  definition, 14
  activities, 61
Family Creed, 57
Farewell, 27
  statement, 54
Feasting, 27
Gifts, 20
Greeters, 24, 28
Greeting, 17
Games, 39-53
Harambee, 18, 26
Hare, Nathan and Julia, 54
Imani
  definition, 14
  activities, 60
Jewlery Club, 55
Karamu Feast, 19, 49
Kibunzi, 23
Kinara,23
  definition, 15
King, Martin Luther, 57
Kikombe
  definition, 16
  cup, 17, 23, 26
Krenga, Maulana, 11
Kujichagulia
  definition, 13
  activities, 59
Kuumba
  definition, 14
  activities, 59
Kwanza, 11
Kwanzaa, 12
  history, 11
  ceremony, 25
  symbols, 15
  Year-round, 45
Libation,
  definition, 17
  statement, 26, 54
Mazao, 23

definition, 15
Mental Olypmics, 50
Mishumaa Saba, 23
definition, 15
Mkeka, 23
definition, 15
National Council of Negro Women, 51
Nia
definition, 14
activities, 57
Nguzo Saba
definition,23
Parks, Rosa, 51
Purpose
definition, 14
activities, 57
Preparation, 29
Program Booklet, 34, 48-9
Rap Sessions, 48
Rites of Passage Program, 54
Rituals, 25
Save up program, 56
Self-Determinition
definition, 13
activities, 51
Seven Principles, 13
Songs, 50-3
Spiritual Expression, 25
Symbols, 15-16
Tamshi la tambiko, 17, 26
Umoja
definition, 13
activities, 48
Ujamaa
definition, 14
activities, 55
Ujima
definition, 13
activities, 53
Unity, 18
definition,13
activity, 48
Vibunzi, 23
definition, 16
Welcoming, 24
Zawadi, 20, 23
definition, 16

THE COMPLETE KWANZAA CELEBRATION BOOK make wonderful holiday gifts. Let us simplify your shopping by sending "The Complete KWANZAA Celebration Book" to anyone in the continental U.S. with a gift card from you.

ORDER FORM

Yes, Please send me ____ KWANZAA Celebration Book(s). Enclosed is my check/ money order for $9.95 per book

(add $ 3.00 for shipping & handling for each order)

NAME________________________________
ADDRESS________________________________
CITY________________STATE__________ZIP__________
PHONE (   )________________________________

❑ *This is a gift, please ship to:*

NAME________________________________
ADDRESS________________________________
CITY________________STATE__________ZIP__________

MESSAGE________________________________
(LOVE, HAPPY KWANZAA, ETC.)
FROM________________________________
(NAME TO APPEAR ON CARD)

All book orders will be sent UPS within 48hrs. of receipt of your check or money order to:

Creative Acrylic Concepts
5792 Kensington Road
Detroit, Michigan 48224

To order by phone call 1-800-524-7134

THE COMPLETE KWANZAA CELEBRATION BASKET is a wonderful resource kit for parents, teachers and other interested in celebrating the Kwanzaa holiday.

Each basket contains:

- *The Complete Kwanzaa Celebration Book* which list over 70 activities to do that support the 7 principles year-round
- Candle Holder/ Kinara (made of natural wood)
- Seven Candles-one representing each Kwanzaa principle
- African Textile Mat-used in the ceremony with laminated finish for easy wipe ups (16 x 22 ins.)
- Straw Basket for fruits and vegetables/ Mazao
- Frankincense & Myrrh Fragrance to set the mood and one
- Ear of Corn symbolizing children in the family.

With "The Complete KWANZAA Celebration Basket" you're sure to create a wonderful family tradition that will be passes on from generation to generation.

Only $49.95

(plus $4.50 shipping and handling)

ORDER FORM

Yes, please send me "The Complete KWANZAA Celebration Basket"
Enclosed is my check /money order for **$49.95**
(add $4.50 to cover shipping and handling for each order)
Name________________________________
Address______________________________
City____________State____________Zip____________
Phone No. ( )____________________________

Send Check or Money Order To:

Creative Acrylic Concepts
5792 Kensington Road
Detroit, MI. 488224
Allow 2-3 WEEKS FOR DELIVERY

To order by phone call 1-800 524-7134

NOTES

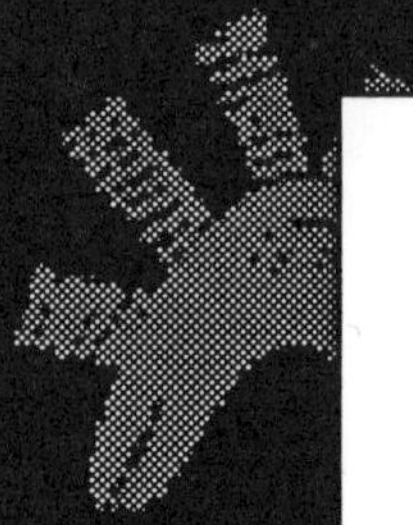

80

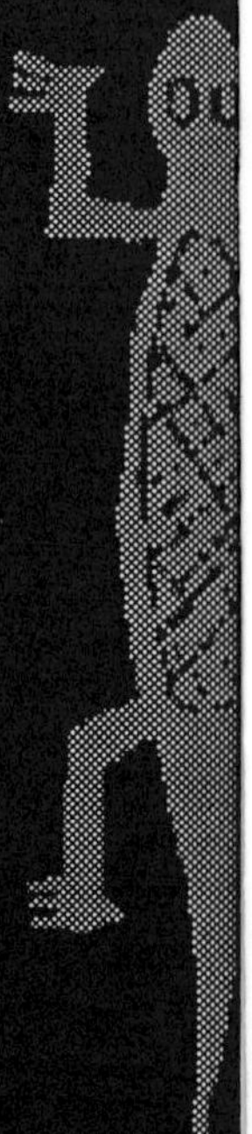